I0456427

From Miss Lady to
FIRST LADY

LaJuanda Sherfield

Copyright © 2024 LaJuanda Sherfield

All rights reserved.

No part of this book may be reproduced, stored in a retrieval system, or transmitted, in any form or by any means, electronic, mechanical, photocopying, recording, or otherwise, without prior written permission from the publisher, except for brief quotations embodied in critical reviews and certain other noncommercial uses permitted by copyright law.

ISBN: 978-1-965666-35-7 (Paperback)

Printed in the United States of America

Contents

Preface

As I washed my face with the hottest water I could stand, trying to exfoliate the guilt and shame of doing what I knew I shouldn't have done. The day has come where my fate is determined by a person in a black robe and a gavel. What will my parents think? What will my church family think? Will my children still love me?

Thank you Niko! I love you! You mean the world to me.

The Assignment

In 2011, I was given the assignment to speak at a Women's Conference. The title was "Victoria isn't the only one with a secret," and my sub-topic was "Don't let the struggle confine you." As I began to speak, I shared a few secrets and struggles that had kept me in bondage because I didn't believe God could use someone like me who had sinned so much. After sharing some of my experiences, I returned to my seat, and the Lord spoke to me and told me to write a book. You would think that I had to write a novel. It took some time. He said other women need to hear your story.

I hope you find encouragement in these pages and never give up hope. I am a living testimony of what God can do through you if you just open your heart to Him.

Chapter 1

How I got the name Miss Lady

I was raised by my grandparents in old-town Virginia. Joe, my grandfather, was six feet tall with a bald head and a rather large nose. He walked with a limp because of a bad hip, and his right index finger was shaped oddly. He told me a squirrel bit it. Wilma, my grandmother, was five foot five with brown skin, a large stomach, and a medium frame with thin lips. She had a quirky sense of humor that only my brother and I could appreciate. They were wonderful grandparents, raising me from infancy to be respectful and well-mannered.

My grandmother insisted I attend church, which I absolutely loved. She would dress me up in a hat, a "pocketbook," as she called it, a dress, a pair of white gloves, and patent leather shoes. Then she would say, "Tuck in your lips," because she had thin lips and thought every woman should do the same lol. She would then exclaim, "Look at Miss Lady! So Sassy!" And that's how I got the nickname Miss Lady. She said I was a little sassy.

As a little girl, I often felt my grandparents were overly strict. I had to stay in front of the yard to play and couldn't go to the playground with the other neighborhood kids. When the streetlights came on, I had to be in the house. Of course, I snuck off sometimes, but Grandma would be waiting at the gate with a wet dishcloth. When I tried sneaking back, she would say, "Come by me," and whack my behind with that dishcloth. She believed in the scripture Proverbs 22:15: "Foolishness is bound up in the heart of a child, but the rod of discipline drives it far from him." When your parents, guardians, or grandparents tell you to stay in the yard, do what they say. There are always consequences for disobedience. There was no time out back then—the only time out was how long she would spank you until she timed out lol.

Now that I'm an adult, I realize I needed all that discipline and those teachings growing up. I thought my life was rather boring because my grandparents wouldn't let me go to friends' houses, attend parties, or do anything fun. They even dressed me like an old lady lol. But I know now they were only protecting me. One thing I loved about my grandparents was how they instilled in me the importance of attending church. I am so glad they put that in me as a little girl. I always loved going to Beulah Baptist Church. I looked forward to the blue and white bus that would pick me up on Sunday mornings. I enjoyed Sunday School. I didn't always understand the preached sermons, but I loved hearing the choir sing. It just did something to me.

There was this choir called the Voices of Supreme. When they sang, it made me feel so good inside. I was inspired by them to join the youth choir. At the time, I was not old enough to join the Voices of Supreme. I was ten years old and had a very heavy voice for a young girl. I had a complex about it because all the other girls' voices were higher than mine. One day, the choir director asked me to sing a solo, "Hold My Hand, Lord." I was so nervous and felt so awkward. I couldn't believe someone with a heavy voice like mine could lead a song. Then I learned that great gospel artists like Albertina Walker and Dorothy Norwood had heavy voices too. Needless to say, I embraced my heavy voice. My sister said my voice was husky lol. After that solo, I was given many more. People at my church would say, "There's something about your voice that makes me cry." They would hug me and say, "Your voice really blesses me." One man even said, "Something about your singing moves me." I didn't understand it then, but today, I know God has anointed my voice. I am not the best singer, but I feel what I sing, and it comes from my heart. I sing to God, not people. To this very day, I'm still singing, and I ask God to let people hear and feel His presence when I sing.

When I grew up, even though I loved church, I didn't like school. I was a little chunky, my hair wasn't the best, and my clothes were definitely outdated. A couple of girls teased me, saying I stank. They would walk around the class, sniffing everyone and stopping at me, saying I was the stinky one. The boys would say I had "beebees" on my neck and make shooting sounds. It was embarrassing, and I was so hurt. These girls, whom I wanted to be like, dressed nicely and had beautiful hair, but they were so mean. I wanted everyone to like me. Kids can be so cruel. When I would go home and tell my grandparents, they would say, "Don't worry about them. You just be the best person, do your work, and come on home." But who understands that in elementary school?

I attended Robert E. Lee, which was right across the street from where I was raised. Then we were bused to Douglas MacArthur. My grandparents were very concerned because, during this time, there was still a lot of racial tension. That area was predominantly white, so my grandparents worried I would not be treated fairly. But it was my own race who treated me badly. I actually liked Douglas MacArthur better than Robert E. Lee. I met new friends who were nice to me. I only had issues with the same girls who teased me, but I still wanted them to like me. I'll never forget one girl in my math class. We had to get into groups to problem-solve. We were discussing something, and she told me to say something really mean about the teacher. Like an idiot, I said it to the group: "The teacher had pooped in her underwear," but I didn't say "pooped" lol.

The girl raised her hand and said, "I said it!" I knew I was in trouble. The teacher removed me from the group while they laughed. The teacher called my grandparents, who called my parents.

I cried and cried because I didn't want to say that, but I really wanted this girl to be my friend. To anyone reading this, if you know anyone like this, get far away from them. I know it's hard at a young age, but the Bible tells me I am fearfully and wonderfully made by God (Psalms 139:14). Jesus loves me, and most importantly, love yourself. Never let anyone make you do what you know is wrong. If people tease you, say, "No weapon formed against me shall prosper, and every tongue which rises against you in judgment you shall condemn" (Isaiah 54:17).

I cried a lot as a kid over the mean things people would say. Today, I know who I am! I am God's masterpiece! Even though I lived with my grandparents, my mom and dad were still in my life. My mom had me at a young age, my grandparents wanted to raise me, and my dad was in the military. It worked out for everyone. Mom would come get me on the weekends. We had so much fun together. We would go shopping, get fashionable clothes, go to Baskin Robbins for our favorite ice cream, and sometimes we would go to the beauty parlor. I learned about the Revlon Perm, lol. We would be in the beauty parlor for hours, but I didn't care.

We would go to my parents' house, play music, and just have fun. I can still hear Earth, Wind & Fire and the Ohio Players. On Saturday night, I would go back to Grandma's. I was so sad! The only music Grandma played was Shirley Caesar's "No Charge," Mahalia Jackson, and the Five Blind Boys of Alabama I like gospel music but the songs

6

were old to me. If you snapped your fingers, it was a sin, lol. If I would dance, Grandma would say, "Ok Miss Lady, sit your frisky self down," lol.

It was hard adjusting to coming back to my grandparents after being with my parents. Back to staying in the yard. One of my uncles would come to see my grandma and grandpa, who were his parents. After visiting with them, he would take me for a ride in his Corvette. I was so happy. My uncle tells the story that I would wave to all the kids in the neighborhood, and afterward, I would fall asleep. That's his story, lol.

As I got older and attended junior high, I went to Minnie Howard, and then transferred to GW Middle School. By the time I got to middle school, I had lost some baby fat. My body began to change. I wasn't teased anymore, but there were many girls who disliked me when I got to middle school because they heard their boyfriends talking about me. I didn't even know this until a new friend I met at GW told me. So I had haters in elementary school, and now in middle school too.

I even had a girl who wanted to fight me because she said I was talking about her mother. Well, I didn't know her, nor did I know her mother. The news got back to me that she was going to beat me up after school. She approached me and said, "I heard you were talking about my mom." Out of fear, I balled up my fist and punched her in the face. Needless to say, after that, I was never teased or hated on again. I could hear everyone saying, "Don't mess with LaJuanda." Afterward, the girl I punched in the face bought me an RC soda, lol. I must admit, I felt good. I am not saying you should go around punching people in the face but enough was enough.

Later on in the school year, I was introduced to a guy by one of my nice friends. He had a moped and played in a band. Even though I was a little older, my grandma didn't allow me to talk to boys on the phone. He asked for my number, but I took his because I knew I would have to sneak and call him. My grandma loved to play bingo. She didn't drive, but she had faithful friends who would pick her up. That was my opportunity to do what I knew I couldn't do around her. So when she would leave, I would call the boy I met. We talked, and he invited me to come hear the band he played in. They were playing right across the street from where I lived.

I ask my Grandma but she said I could not attend. Well, the night the band played was a bingo night. Grandma would be gone for a minimum of three hours, so I figured I would wait until her friends picked her up and sneak over to the recreation center and get back before she got home. My grandfather was home, but he was asleep in his chair or watching 'Gunsmoke' or something. I got past my grandfather and went to the recreational center. I saw a lot of people from my school there. Everyone was dancing, laughing, and having a great time. I began to bop my head a little. I wasn't much of a dancer, but I would move my shoulders a lot. I saw some friends, and we were talking and joking around. Before I knew it, three hours had passed. It was dark in the recreation center, so I didn't know what time it was. I was having fun. While I was dancing, I heard over the PA system, "LaJuanda, front and center." I heard it again. Then I heard, "Cut these lights on in here. My granddaughter is in here." I wished I could have disappear. How she knew I was at the recreational center, I will never know. She was wearing a blue polyester coat with some ugly brown slides and pink hair rollers.

When I walked to that door, I was so embarrassed, lol. I knew I was about to be ridiculed at school, and the boy I liked would never talk to me again. Grandma and I walked home, and she was really upset. She told me to get in the house, and I wouldn't be going anywhere anytime soon. Ephesians 6:1: "Obey your parents in the Lord." God is always watching so even when you think no one is watching, God is."

The morning conversation that Monday at the bus stop was, "Your grandma came and got you from the rec." They laughed at me, and after a while, I laughed too! I was still trying to figure out how she knew where I was. Back in those days, neighborhood watch was everybody your parents knew. They even had permission to spank you if necessary. Someone probably watching me told my grandma they saw me leaving because everyone knew I could not go out of the yard, or I had to be right in front.

I decided to join the Pep Club at school. I thought it would get me out of the house without getting in trouble. I wanted to be a cheerleader, but Grandma said the uniform was too short and I should not be showing all my legs. The Pep Club were cheerleaders with clothes on. We would be the hype squad at the basketball games. Our coach would teach us all about the facts of life, how to take care of our bodies, and what to expect from boys.

As I continued to grow up as a teenager, I really wanted to be with my mom. I felt like Grandma didn't understand my growing up. I started to like boys. I wanted to talk on the phone, not just to boys but to my girlfriends too. I wanted to hang out with my friends a little more, but Grandma was not having it. I had a conversation with my mom and asked if I could come stay with her, and she said yes. By this time, my mom and dad were divorced. My mom had a boyfriend, and my grandma was so disappointed because I wanted my mom. I loved my grandma, and I still miss her a lot! I miss the funny things she would say, like "Tain while," which meant never mind. She would tell me to "cut the lights out in the Jice," which was the ceiling. If I hurt myself, she would say, "It will get better before you get married." If I asked where she was going, she would say, "To see the Duck Tech Water," and I can't forget, "Don't drink coffee because it makes you black," lol.

I totally understand now why my grandparents were strict and protective. They didn't want any harm to come to me, and real love protects. I know now they were only looking out for me. I didn't like the discipline or corrections, but it was necessary, and it's definitely needed today. Proverbs 22:15: "Foolishness is bound in the heart of a child, but the rod of correction shall drive it far from him." Even as adults, correction and discipline are necessary; it helps us to grow. The Bible tells us that open rebuke is better than secret love. If we get disciplined in front of others, maybe it will scare us enough that we will not do that same thing again.

Chapter 2

Moving to Maryland

I moved to Maryland with my mom and her boyfriend. Moving to Maryland wasn't bad, but I felt bad for my Grandma because She raised me from infancy, despite her strictness and overly protectiveness I knew She would miss me and I would miss her. However, I was excited to live with my mom.

I was a latchkey kid. I called my mom when I left and returned home from school. We lived on the third floor of an apartment with a balcony, which I thought was so cool at the time lol.

My mom and her boyfriend had rules in place for me. I would do my homework and chores, then wait for my mom to get home. My mom and her boyfriend set rules for me. I must admit, I didn't always follow them lol. My mom told me I couldn't have friends over, and for a while, I didn't. But as I made new friends in our apartment complex, I wanted to fit in. As a teen, everybody wants to fit in. Everybody wants someone to like them and although at this time I didn't have problems with meeting people and making new friends.

My problem was being obedient to what my mom and her boyfriend said.

Despite my mom's rules, I started having friends over. We would listen to albums on the stereo set lol, even though I wasn't supposed to touch it I had to play my favorite album which was Parliament. And the song "Flashlight" was a hit among us. We had so much fun dancing and joking around, but I never thought about the consequences If I was caught. I did have some friends that would look up the hallway where we lived in the apartment complex to see if my mom and dad were on their way into the complex there was a window that was in the hallway that you could see cars coming through so I would have a look out person but I was being disobedient, let me tell you something you cannot continue to keep doing the wrong thing it will catch up with you because what we think a mom and a dad and people don't see God sees everything so guess what? I got caught!

I didn't have a lookout person this particular day, so what I did was open the door quickly and I told another one of my friends to just to warn me if my parents were coming. Suddenly, I heard them approaching. In a panic, I tried to hide my friends. I managed to get one friend to run across the hall to another apartment, but I couldn't hide the other. I told her to go out on the balcony and stay there until my parents went to their room. I would let her back in when they left lol. However, that particular day my mom and dad stayed out in the front room for ever which they normally did not do, they usually would stay in their bedroom. but today was different for some reason so I'm panicking because I know that this girl was outside on the balcony, and before I knew it, hours had passed And this girl was still out on the balcony.

Eventually, she knocked on the balcony door. My mom heard the tap, tap, tap and went to open it. When she saw my friend say, "LaJuanda left me out here." My mom called me out of my room and asked me to explain. I don't remember what I told her, but my friend was able to go home. Once she left, I knew I was in big trouble.

My mom told me to go to my room. Then she noticed the turntable still spinning. Before I knew it, my mom's size 10 shoe was in my behind. I was shocked. The cool mom I loved so much had punished me. She grounded me, no phone, no going outside. I could only leave my room to go to the bathroom and eat dinner.

I learned a valuable lesson: what you do in the dark comes to the light. When you get punished for doing something wrong, those are just the consequences. Ask God to forgive you and don't do it again.

I stopped having friends over after realizing how much it broke my mom's heart and how disappointed she was at my disobedience. I never wanted my mom to be mad at me. Even though she was upset, I knew she still loved me. (Side note: God is like our parent. When we do things that displease Him, He corrects us, but He still loves us.)

I continued visiting my grandparents on the weekends because I attended church. It wasn't bad going back on weekends; in fact, I missed my grandparents. My grandfather was always cooking some delicious food lol. On Saturdays, I attended choir rehearsal, and a few friends from the Southside were in the choir too. It was a chance to see them and keep up with the latest happenings in Virginia. Shout out to the Southside Family!

One of my poor choices while visiting my grandparents was learning to shoplift. A few girls I associated with would go to stores and steal. I watched them get away with so many items, and eventually, I tried it myself. To my surprise, it worked. I became so good at it that I would go to stores by myself to shoplift.

You might wonder how I got there. In Old Town VA, where my grandparents lived, there was a bus stop. While visiting Wilma and Joe, I would meet my friends at the bus stop. My friends taught me which bus to catch. I continued shoplifting until I almost got caught. I will never forget that day at a store called Woodies. I had a large, deep purse and picked up several IZOD pieces. I went to the dressing room, placed them all in my purse, and left. As I was leaving, I heard security describe a young black girl with purple and white clothing heading to the front door. Even in my wrongdoings, God was still covering me. When I heard that, I immediately dropped the purse with the stolen items and ran out of the store towards the bus. One of the boys from church saw me running while driving by, and called my name. He asked me what I was doing and why I was running. I don't remember what I told him, but he told me to hop in his car. That was one of the scariest days of my life. I kept thinking about what my mom and grandmother would think if the police had caught me. I would never see the outside world again lol. After that, I asked God for forgiveness and never shoplifted again.

I don't know what got into me. This is why your friends matter. If I weren't in that environment, I would never have thought to do what I did. The scripture clearly says, "Thou shalt not steal" (Exodus 20:15). If you do steal, lie, or cheat, 1 John 1:9 says, "If we confess our sins, He is faithful and just to forgive our sins and to cleanse us from all unrighteousness." My advice to anyone now would be to pray and ask God to put good friends in your circle. If you have to be by yourself until God gives you the right friends it's ok. Your right now decisions work for your future.

I attended a new middle school called Lord Baltimore. I liked it and met many new friends. One girl in particular, named Tutti, was very friendly and made me feel comfortable. When she asked my name, I said LaJuanda. She thought it was too long and asked if I had a nickname lol. I said no, but my mom calls me Fatty. From that day on, I was "Fatty," and everyone called me that until I left middle school for high school. Do you see the influence of one person? Imagine what one believer in Christ could do by spreading the gospel, which is the good news of Christ. In Romans 1:16, Paul said, "I am not ashamed of the gospel of Christ, for it is the power of God unto salvation to everyone that believes."

So, Fatty became quite popular, and I found myself surrounded by many cute boys. They noticed me, and I noticed them. I got into a lot of trouble talking to some of these boys. I won't lie; I liked the attention. But now I know it was for the wrong reasons. The boys who liked me were interested in one thing, and that hasn't changed today. I didn't know my value or worth and allowed people to treat me like I was on the clearance rack. Sadly, I gave myself up too soon. I didn't value who I was or recognize that my body is the temple of God, nor did I understand the consequences of premature actions.

You are worth the wait, sister or brother. Wait until you're married. Sex was designed by God, so it's not a bad thing, but the world's system has distorted and taken advantage of intimacy before marriage. Premature sex is dangerous because it involves various spirits that each of you have come in contact with. You have to ask God to cleanse you from all spirits you have allowed to enter your body. This is why some of you feel depressed, weird, crazy, and desire things that are not of God. These spirits have been deposited. Say to God, "Create in me a clean heart and renew the right spirit in me." You can find this in the book of Psalms, chapter 51, verses 10-12. God will cleanse you and make you clean.

There was also an attempted rape when I was young. I was coming home from a recreation event, and someone apparently followed me. He came up behind me, picked me up, and threw me down the stairs of a building. He tried really hard to get my pants down while I fought back with all my strength. He began to unzip my pants, but I had an umbrella in my hand, and I hit him with it repeatedly until he left me alone. I felt horrible and remember crying and crying. The worst part of this story is that when I went to a family member and told them what had happened, they didn't believe me. I showed them my dirty coat from being on the floor, and they still didn't believe me.

I cried so hard I could hardly breathe. I knew the person who tried to rape me and went to their family, but they didn't believe me either because I was young. You can't imagine how I felt. That wound never healed until my relationship with Christ became strong.

If this has happened to you, it's not your fault. Bad things happen because of the sin in this world. God will heal your broken heart and give you recompense for all your troubles. You can move forward and not let the enemy make you think that people who do bad things or even the bad things you have done, can stop the plans God has for you. Jeremiah 29:11 says, "For I know the thoughts that I think toward you, saith the Lord, thoughts of peace and not of evil, to give you an expected end." So forgive the person who hurt you physically, mentally, and emotionally. God is close to the brokenhearted, as stated in Psalms 34:18-19.

It's really important in our youth to read and study the Bible. Meditate on the word and apply it to your daily life. It will keep you in perfect peace when your mind is stayed on Him. The Bible in John 16:33 says that in this life we will have trials and troubles. I would rather have Jesus with me in my troubles than be without Him.

Chapter 3

Highschool

While finishing up my middle school years at Lord Baltimore, my counselor informed me of an opportunity to attend a trade school for high school. I had to be selected for a particular trade, and I chose Cosmetology because I aspired to be a hair stylist. At that time, only two students were selected from each middle school in the area, and guess who made the cut? Yes, it was me, Fatty. Instead of attending Friendly High School, I would go to Gwynn Park Senior High School's Trade and Industrial Program. The school was much farther from home, requiring me to catch the bus at 6:15 am. It was a short bus. You already know I was cooked lol. Needless to say, I got teased a lot for that, and my family still jokes about it. Maybe it explains why I'm just a little bit "touched," lol.

Cosmetology was so much fun. We had to complete 1,500 hours over three years. Afterward, we had to take a state board exam with a model and wait for the results. My choir director, Ms. Cathy, was my model—shout out to her. I passed with flying colors and became a licensed cosmetologist. I did hair for a while, often going to clients' homes, my church family supported me. However, I didn't stick with it because I lacked confidence and constantly compared myself to other stylists who had been in the business longer. I never felt I could be as good as they were. Let this be a lesson: compare yourself to no one. You were designed to be you. If God has given you a gift or talent, do your best and do it wholeheartedly, as unto the Lord (Colossians 3:23).

High school was an amazing time. I met some wonderful friends in Cosmetology. We called ourselves the Fabulous Five—shout out to Dana, Charlie, Wyona, and Kay. I still remember changing into our white uniforms for class. Those were the good old days. I was pretty popular in high school and talked a lot, always having a corny joke ready for my friends each morning. I was very friendly and had no drama during those years. I met a boy who was good at basketball and exceptional at track, especially high jumping. We exchanged greetings in the hallway, and eventually, we became boyfriend and girlfriend. Sadly, he has since passed away, and I want to show respect to his memory.

Here's a funny story about our relationship. We dated for two years and even got engaged. He gave me a nice ring, which I proudly showed to my parents. They kept saying it was too light to be a real engagement ring, but I didn't care. Exactly two weeks later, the ring began to turn green. I called him and asked for the receipt so we could exchange it, but he never gave it to me. I nagged him for two weeks about the ring, and he finally confessed that he bought it at KMART, LOL! Now I understood why it turned colors. I'll never forget the ugly yellow electric 225 he wanted me to ride in. He was a funny, good guy. Rest in peace, Kade. I can laugh now lol. We didn't stay together much longer after that but remained good friends. I have fond memories of high school.

I graduated in 1984. I wanted to go to college but didn't have the money and knew nothing about financial aid and grants. My parents didn't know either, so I worked in several salons. I learned a lot and knew I could have gone further in the hair industry, but I just didn't believe in myself.

Chapter 3

After Graduating

After graduating in May 1984, I didn't have a concrete plan for my life. Instead, I started going out with a guy named Jay, who had once picked me up when I was almost caught shoplifting. Jay was extremely nice and kind, and we had a lot of fun together. I knew his parents from church; his father was a pastor who could both sing and preach. In fact, it was his father who sort of pushed us to go out with each other. It was Jay's dad who asked if his son could get my number. We would talk on the phone and go out. Jay had a big heart, and his friends knew it. He would drive them anywhere since he had a car, essentially becoming a taxi service for them. They would pay him with a nickel bag, as I don't remember anyone ever putting gas in the car.

We ended up getting married in November 1984 because I didn't want to stay in the house with my mom and stepdad at the time. My stepdad was very strict, even after I graduated and turned 18, and I wanted out. To my readers, this is not the way to do it. Ironically, I wanted to escape my parents' home, but we ended up moving in with his parents. Crazy, right? Lol. When planning to get married, have a plan, a good job, save your money so you can at least get your own place. You may have to rent at first, but save for that down payment on your home. Most importantly, let the Holy Spirit lead you.

Moving in with his parents wasn't too bad except Jay thought it was okay to leave me at home with them rather than spend time with me. His friends became priority. I had some good conversations with Ms. Lea and Rev. They have both since passed away. But we had just gotten married; shouldn't we have been in marital bliss? This continued for a while, and about eight months later, we moved into our own apartment. By then, we both had pretty good jobs. We only had one car, so Jay would have to drive me to work and pick me up.

This wasn't an issue until, after picking me up, we had to pick up his trifling friends. Yes, I called them trifling. All his friends would now hang out at our apartment, smoking. I hate the smell of smoke and weed to this day. People who smoke aren't aware of how bad they smell after a cigarette or weed; it makes me want to throw up. Just about every day, people were over at our apartment smoking. I was so annoyed. It got so bad that if I had a day off work, Jay would have his friends come to the apartment and wait until he got home just to smoke. I was young and didn't want to hurt anyone's feelings, but now I realize I shouldn't have let them in. Who would allow their friends to come to their home while their wife is there? This shows how immature we were.

One day, his friends were in the kitchen, and I went to my room. I remember hearing pots and pans and smelling something really weird. All I could hear from my room was, "Hurry up, man, that is enough; let me hit." I walked out of my room and tipped into the living room, peeking into the kitchen without them seeing me. They were cooking and smoking what I now know to be crack. I was shocked. I had never seen grown men argue over how long it was taking to pass the crack pipe. I went back to my room and heard the door. Jay was now home and joined them in the kitchen. I was so disappointed to know that he participated in this awful substance. Our apartment was all smoked up, and it was the worst smell.

While they continued to smoke, one of Jay's friends tried to come to me in my room and get me to smoke the pipe. I called Jay to get his friend, but he was so blasted from that stuff he didn't even respond. I just cried and said, "Lord, what did I get into? How did I end up with a person who does drugs?" When the drugs ran out, they all left. This continued for a while until I was fed up. I tried having a conversation about his addiction and his friends, but he wouldn't let them go. I will never forget him saying his friends were there before me. That was the straw that broke the camel's back. I called my dad and left. I went back home with my parents. I didn't even mention that Jay tried to sell drugs, but it didn't work out because he and his friends smoked the product and couldn't account for the money that was due for those drugs. I began to get fearful. By the time I left, he had a strong addiction to weed and Love Boat, which started to alter his behavior. I, along with his family, tried to help him and suggested he go into a treatment program, but he refused. Even though I left the marriage, I always prayed for him. I learned that only God can help and change a person. Never stop praying. The Bible tells us we should pray without ceasing.

After being back home, I started to feel really sick. Everything and everyone stank, and I was super nauseous. I went to the doctor, and they told me the rabbit died. That's what they used to say back in the day if your pregnancy test was positive. I was six weeks pregnant. I craved crab legs, IHOP pancakes, and watermelon. My mom was so supportive; she would get up in the middle of the night to get pancakes because that's what the baby wanted, lol. I must admit I caught a lot of flack from people because I separated from Jay. I really thought this was the best thing for me. I didn't feel safe anymore. Once I knew I was carrying a little life inside, I needed peace and refused to be stressed while carrying my child. I wanted a healthy pregnancy, and the environment I was in while married was not a good place. I got a job at a hotel while I was pregnant. My mom would drop me off. I would throw up all the time. I had morning sickness like you wouldn't believe lol. My hair grew long, and my skin was glowing; everyone thought I was so beautiful. The hotel I worked for looked out for me. They made sure I ate well and got lots of rest. One guy wanted to date me. I said, "I'm flattered, but you see this belly?" He didn't care. I even told him I was separated but still legally married. He said, "So? You're beautiful." I said, "Let's see how I'm feeling after I have my baby." I had no intentions of getting back with Jay; I just wanted him to be delivered. He was a good guy who made some bad choices, like all of us have done. The Bible says in Romans 3:23, "We all have sinned and fallen short." I hold no judgment. God is good; he delivered Jay from drugs, and he is now born again.

Chapter 5

My first Child

Three weeks before delivering, I took off work to relax and prepare for the blessing God allowed me to carry. In August 1987, as I was about to perm my hair, a rush of water came gushing out. I told my mom my water broke. We called the doctor, but I wasn't going anywhere until I put that Revlon in my hair. Thinking a pad would hold the water, I soon realized it was no match. Determined, I sat on the floor and applied the perm, then prepared to go to the hospital. My mom helped me with everything. We notified all the family and headed to Alexandria Hospital.

After getting settled in my room, I had a few contractions but was not dilating. The baby was in distress, and we had to act quickly, so I had a C-section. At 11:32 pm, a beautiful baby girl, Tiffany Chanel, was born, weighing 6 pounds and 19 ounces. Children are truly a gift from God. Seeing this beautiful little person was a miracle. We stayed in the hospital for five days, and every nurse adored Tiffany; she was the cutest little girl. I remember going to the nursery and panicking when she wasn't in her little bed. The nurses had her at the station, holding and cuddling her. After that, I kept my baby right next to me.

When the photographer came to take pictures of the newborns, I dressed Tiffany in a pink outfit with a bow in her hair. She was too cute for the hospital t-shirt. When we were released from the hospital, we went straight to my baby shower and then home. It didn't really hit me until I got home that I was a mom. I was now responsible for raising this precious baby God had loaned me. She was a good baby, but not a good sleeper; she woke up every hour and a half. Despite the sleepless nights, she brought so much joy to our family. I stayed home for eight weeks before returning to work at the hotel. Leaving her was hard, but she was in good hands with my mom.

Chapter 6

Back to Work

Going back to work was incredibly hard. The bond you form with your newborn is amazing—you lose a lot of sleep and change countless diapers, but it's so rewarding being a parent. For those who don't have children, you can still be the greatest mom or dad. Don't be discouraged; you can be the best version of a parent and a blessing to those whose biological parents aren't meeting their needs. God has given you the gift to be that non-live-in parent.

After returning to work, the guy I mentioned earlier was still pursuing me. He was glad I was back, and we worked in the same area of the hotel. I told my supervisor that he wanted to go out with me, and she saw nothing wrong with it. So, I went out with him. He treated me like a queen, opening doors, paying for meals and movies. He always bought me things—flowers, even though I never liked them, and even a car. I must admit, I liked the attention. We continued to go out and decided to become a couple. It was totally wrong because I was still legally married. You should not date until your divorce is final or you become a widow.

The relationship was really good initially, so I let him meet Tiffany. He liked her a lot and bought her everything from milk to clothes and toys. He even gave her the nickname "Duck." One day, I decided that Tiffany should be dedicated, and that's when my nice guy turned into a nightmare. He didn't think Tiffany's dad should be a part of the dedication because he wasn't active in her life at that time. I will never forget, we were at his parents' house discussing it, and he got so mad he pulled out a knife on me and threatened me. Needless to say, I was terrified and just cried. His parents tried to calm him down, but he was outraged. He felt that since he was doing so much for Tiffany, he should be the only one there.

After the storm of Dee calmed down, we left. I was trembling and praying all the way home. I didn't know what he would do to us. Out of fear, I stayed with him. We finally got to my house; I had moved from my parents to a little place my grandfather let me use while he was out of town. Dee apologized, and I said okay, but I went to make a bath for Tiffany and me. Several minutes later, he called and asked if I loved him. I hesitated to answer because I was still upset about what he did at his parents' house. Before I knew it, he grabbed me and dragged me through the house until I said I loved him. He threatened to drown me if I didn't say it. Tiffany was in the other room. I said, "I love you," and he let me go. I was in total disbelief, trying to figure out who this guy was. He had turned into Dr. Jekyll.

I checked on Tiffany, who was just laying in her crib. I grabbed her and tried to figure out how to get away, but I just couldn't think straight. We never took a bath because I couldn't trust Dee not to try to drown us. Anytime he did something crazy, he would say there would be consequences if I told anyone, so I kept this dark secret inside. We finally went to sleep. Dee apologized again, and I would say okay, but I never believed he was truly sorry. I stayed in this abusive relationship until I had a solid plan. I prayed and asked God for a way out. When I woke up the next day, my body was sore from him dragging me. After this situation, I was quiet—anyone who knows me knows I'm not usually quiet. I only said the bare minimum to him from this point.

It was really hard to get away from him because we worked together. I wanted to tell people at work, but I didn't know what he would do. It's really hard to write about this part of my life. He did a lot of crazy stuff to me. Sometimes, if we were riding together, he would take me to a dark road, make me get out of the car, and leave me there. He would come back laughing while I was crying my eyes out. I remember one time, we were going to visit my grandma. Tiffany was with us, and he pulled over at a gas station, took Tiffany out of her car seat, and held her upside down outside the driver's window. I started screaming, "Give me my baby," and he threatened to drop her unless I said I loved him more than her. Of course, I said I loved him to get him to stop swinging my baby. He lifted her back up and gave her to me. I was thankful she wasn't crying. I hugged and kissed her, put her back in her seat, and asked nicely if he could take me to my grandmother's. I am so thankful to God for His protection over Tiffany and me. God was a very present help in the time of trouble (Psalms 46:10).

Once Dee took me to my grandmother's, I stayed there. The only thing I regretted was that he knew where my grandmother lived. I left my place and the car he bought me. This was my way out. The Bible talks about the way of escape (I Corinthians 10:13). My next plan was to quit my job so I didn't have to ever see him again. I saw him at work that Monday or Tuesday, and he asked why I hadn't been home. I told him I decided my grandmother needed me, so I would stay with her. He asked about us, and I told him I couldn't stay in the relationship because he scared me. He apologized and said he shouldn't treat me like that. So, we parted ways. I got a new job and took the bus to and from work. My grandmother Wilma watched Tiffany. One evening, I got home and walked into my grandmother's yard when someone came up behind me. It was Dee. I said, "Oh no!" He said, "It's just me." I thought something is really wrong with this dude, he is stalking me now. "Dude you're crazy for real." Needless to say, I rushed him off really fast.

Ladies, we must be careful with who we date, times change. If you have children, don't let them meet who you're dating for at least 6 months.

People are crazy. I would rather stay by myself than go through what I went through. I owe God praise because He sent angels to watch over me and Tiffany. Time passed, and Dee called me at my grandmother's. I don't recall how he got the number. He told me he was going into the military as an airborne ranger. He said the Lord told him if he didn't get it right with me and Tiffany, he would die when he jumped. This time, I believed him. I felt like this was for real. So, he bought Tiffany a lot of stuff, and I let him pick us up. We went back to his parents, where he apologized. We had a nice dinner, and he took me back to my grandmother's. We never heard from him again.

After some time, I was leaving a church service one evening. On my way to the car, I saw a guy named Will, who grew up with my family, but I hadn't seen him in years because he was in prison. We talked for a long time about what happened to him and I shared what I had been going through. It was getting late so we exchanged numbers and said we would keep in touch. It was several months later when we met up for lunch on a Saturday. We kept hanging out, going to parks and sometimes the club. Will was a smooth talker, he was tall, handsome, very slim, and dressed nicely. He knew how to get the ladies. He was always telling me to watch his moves. Time goes by and he tells me that he has feelings for me. I responded by saying we are like family and we can't get together and I left it at that. We continued to hang out with each other. We would have fun; no pressure, just hanging out, playing cards with some of his friends.

As time goes by I eventually begin to get feelings for Will. We even started going to church together. He told me he was tired of playing the field and he wanted a family. He had children but he said he didn't want any more kids without doing it the right way. We later got an apartment and got married. We had a little boy who we named Dante Jeremiah 7 pounds, 9 oz. 8 months after Dante was born, Will died of cancer (Lymphoma) at 31 years of age. This was really hard on me. I never imagined becoming a widow at such a young age. It was only God's grace that I was able to get through such a painful experience. My family was a great support system as well.

Chapter 7

The Trial!!

I was tired of working weekends and holidays and wanted to spend more time with my kids. So, I opened a daycare in my home. It went okay for a while, but I didn't have enough children to bring in the income I needed. Eventually, I got hired as a payroll assistant. It was a good-paying job with benefits, and I could set my own hours. It was sweet. After learning how to process payroll, I noticed employees had loan deductions taken out of their pay. I decided to take a loan, but without permission. When I realized how easy it was, I continued to loan myself money that didn't belong to me.

This went on for a while until I was convicted that it was wrong. The Bible tells us that we should not steal, so I began to pay back what I had borrowed from the company. I thought I could return it all before anyone noticed or before an audit. But apparently, it was too late. One day, I was called to HR and asked if I had been taking money. I admitted to it and took full responsibility for my actions. I was very sorry. At that time, I was a young widow, and initially, everything was fine with the money until it wasn't. I allowed the enemy to convince me that I could do this and not get caught. Needless to say, I was terminated from a great job with excellent benefits.

I thought that was the end, but a few days later, I was served court papers. I didn't tell anyone about this. I talked to God, told Him how sorry I was, and asked for His forgiveness. I promised never to do anything like that again, and I meant it. This secret made me so sick. I was overwhelmed with guilt and shame. Even though I asked God to forgive me, I couldn't forgive myself for making such a bad decision and not thinking about the consequences. I kept thinking about what would happen if I went to jail and lost my kids. I thought about how embarrassed my family would be.

The sin I committed was so devastating to me that I stopped eating. I was depressed and weak, barely able to get out of bed. I saw my own funeral and immediately heard God say, "Be still and know that I am God." I had to trust that even in my wrong, God would never leave or forsake me. It's in His word (Hebrews 13:5), and God is not a man to lie (Numbers 23:19). I went to live with a friend of mine. I didn't tell her anything at the time. The guilt and shame consumed me and made me feel worthless. My friend noticed how sick I looked and called the mother of the church I would attend from time to time. She prayed for me and also called my mother. They thought I had a bad case of the flu.

Later that evening, I rolled out of bed and crawled to the bathroom. I found enough strength to hold on to the sink and look in the mirror. I said, "Devil, I made a mistake, but Jesus justified me at the cross. You will no longer play tricks in my head, making me sick and making me think I won't be here for my children. God has forgiven me. I am a conqueror. I will go through and come out as pure gold. I will face my Goliath." I told myself, "I am redeemed. I am the righteousness of God. I am forgiven." I repeated this every day.

Even in your wrong, God is so merciful and forgiving. Jesus went to the cross for all our sins. Romans 5:8 says, "But God shows His love for us in that while we were still sinners, Christ died for us." All we have to do is repent and turn from our wicked ways.

I went to court for a hearing with evidence to charge me with embezzlement. I was 31, a widow with two kids, facing a bad decision that could cost me prison time. After the hearing, I went back home and got sicker and sicker, still keeping this secret. I was too afraid to tell anyone because I felt like an embarrassment to my family. I cried every night until the next court date. I was assigned a court-appointed lawyer. All I remember doing was asking God to have mercy on me. My lawyer said that since it was my first offense, I would probably get five years or less. I thought, "How am I going to tell my kids I'm going to jail?" She said I might get probation; it depended on the judge.

On the day of the trial in May 1997, while dressing for court, I wrote on a piece of paper: Romans 3:23: "We all have sinned and fallen short of the glory of God." On another piece of paper, I wrote: "We walk by faith and not by sight." I wanted to go to court standing and walking on the word. I kept telling myself, "I am forgiven." In the courtroom, the judge sentenced everyone who had a case to jail. I thought, "This judge doesn't play." My case was scheduled early, but it wasn't called until 3:15. I believe it was a test to see if I would trust God to work on my behalf.

Finally, they called my case. The charge was presented to the judge. My attorney fought for me, saying I was a good person who made a bad decision. She emphasized that I was a widow with two kids who fell on hard times. The prosecutor argued that I was wrong and should be sentenced to jail, regardless of it being my first offense. She went on and on. I prayed, "Lord, I need You to work this courtroom right now and silence this prosecutor. You know how sorry I am." Less than a minute later, the judge said, "Five years, but I will suspend them all as long as she does 200 hours of community service, probation, and pays restitution." I said, "Thank you, Jesus! Thank you, Your Honor." God truly is a lawyer in the courtroom.

I had to make arrangements with the court, and I was out of there. What a relief! I know God loves me, and He loves you too. After this, I rededicated my life to Christ. Not because I was so good, but because God is so good. I am a witness that God can take your mess and turn it into a message. I was able to do my community service at church and stayed on probation for five years. I was okay with that—it wasn't jail. I also had to pay restitution. I was ashamed of telling anyone, but God told me to share my story in a book because others need to know my testimony. I was ashamed, but I am free. I want you to be free. Everyone makes mistakes; your mistake may not be what I did, but ask God to forgive you and mean it. Don't go back to the wrong. Move forward. Your past is just that—your past. You're not defined by your past. Don't let people tell you otherwise unless you're still wrong. When you repent, people should see the new you because Repentance brings change. Be honest with God and yourself. Your heart must be sincere. There is nothing new under the sun. Sin was here before we got here; this is why God sent His son Jesus. He died and rose because He loves us. Don't worry about people; we have to answer to God. Respect people, but they are not our Creator. We are to live a life that pleases Him. Some people may still have a hard time accepting you after they know your past. Don't worry about it. You can show them how you're changing or have changed with love. Even in all your mistakes, God can still use you because He sees your end during the beginning and the middle.

It was in this trying moment of my life that the Lord told me I was called to be an Evangelist. Of course, I questioned it. But this scripture in John let me know I was okay: John 15:16: "Ye have not chosen me, but I have chosen you and ordained you." Have you read the Bible? Looked at all the great leaders in the Bible? Paul used to kill Christians, Moses killed a man, David had Uriah killed, Jacob was a trickster. Don't let the devil make you think God can't use you. That is exactly what he wants. If he can keep you in guilt and shame, you won't fulfill your purpose. It was a lesson learned, and now you can share how much God loves you. We need to share our testimony. Don't be ashamed—be free! "And they have conquered him by the blood of the lamb and by the word of their testimony." (Revelations 12:11)

Chapter 8

Dead Marriage

My neighbor, whom I miss dearly, told me about a guy in Connecticut who made good money and was looking to date. It had been some years since I dated, so I decided to talk to him. We spoke on the phone every night, and he seemed like a very nice guy. He said he had his own condo and worked for an engineering company, making good money. I thought that was great because I had never met anyone who was an engineer. After talking on the phone for several months, he sent me money to take a train to meet him, as I didn't want to fly at the time.

When I met him, he had beautiful green eyes but the ugliest car, lol. He picked me up from the train station, and we went out for dinner. After dinner, we went back to his condo, which was very nice, but I kept thinking this car is so ugly lol. After going back to his home, we watched something on television, but mostly we just talked, as we had done on the phone every night. The following day, I took a train back to Virginia. The relationship continued on the phone for a while, and he would send me money to take care of me and my kids and pay my bills. I was impressed because I didn't ask him for money; he just did it.

Eventually, I decided to give the relationship a try because this man had money. However, this is never the reason to marry. Yes, you can buy what you want and pay all the bills, but inside, you're still lonely, longing for peace and happiness. At this point in my life, my peace was everything. He eventually asked me to marry him, and I said yes. He asked where we could get married. I was working at a Memorial Park at the time and mentioned to a coworker that I was getting married but didn't have a place. Instead of my church or a nice venue, I got married for the third time in a cemetery, at a beautiful fountain called the Fountain of Youth. A normal person would have thought, "It's a graveyard!" My family probably thought I was crazy, but they supported me.

We moved to Connecticut about a month or two after the wedding. One day, the phone rang, and I answered it. The caller said the rent was three months behind. I was shocked because I thought he owned the condo. I explained that I had just gotten married and didn't know about the overdue rent. Please don't evict us while my kids and I are here. While cleaning the condo, I found big bottles of alcohol hidden under every cabinet. That was the final straw. When my husband got home, I questioned him about the call and the alcohol. He denied everything. I didn't argue; I just continued to move in silence. The next morning, I called my parents to come get me. Needless to say, this marriage was dead from the start.

After that experience, I said I was not dating again. How many times do we say we won't do something again, only to do it again and again? Even though we keep doing what we know is wrong, God's mercy covers us every time. We may face consequences we don't want to deal with, but Christ gives us chance after chance. Romans 7:19 says, "For the good that I would do, I do not; but the evil which I would not, that I do."

I moved back to Woodbridge, Virginia. I started to feel a little depressed about another failed marriage. And I still felt the hurt of losing Walt. I never seek counseling, I was praying. But I just wanted to laugh and have fun so I started going to clubs a lot—not to look for a guy like some do, but because I loved the sound of good music. I enjoyed dancing, even though I wasn't a great dancer. I could move my shoulders pretty well, and when Frankie Beverly's "Before I Let Go" and Craig Mack came on, I would cut a step. I was never a drinker or smoker. I tried drinking once—Cisco, which tasted like orange soda. But orange soda doesn't make you fall out and give you a hangover so bad that even the sound of a door closing hurts. I was miserable and never drank Cisco again. I tried wine coolers but never finished them. I'm so glad I never got addicted. I never smoked cigarettes, and I tried weed but didn't like it. It made me feel like I had no control over my body. I didn't like that feeling, and cigarettes and weed stink. The smell lingers in your clothes, hair, house, and car, and if you have kids, they smell like smoke too. If you're smoking, be mindful of how the smell lingers. God can take that desire away from you if you ask Him, but you have to want to stop and get to the root of why you're so dependent on these substances.

As my life continued on a downward spiral, I got into relationships that I knew were unhealthy. I bought a house and then lost it. I stopped going to church like I should and took a job that required me to work weekends and nights, which took me out of church completely. But it's funny, I still had time to go to clubs. My priorities were all messed up. And the club was my coping mechanism.

Then I met a well-known comedian in the DMV area at a club, and he introduced me to his manager, who looked like Frankie Beverly. I was thrilled to meet him. He was the sweetest, nicest guy. We hooked up for a while and even went on trips out of town. It's crazy how blinded we can be when we're hurt and broken. He could have done anything to me, but he didn't. Thank God. Remember, if

38

you're going out with someone, they might start off nice, but you have to be on guard because we live in a different time, and people are crazy. But this Frankie Beverly look-alike treated me like a queen. Anything I wanted, I had.

One weekend, I don't remember exactly where we were, but we were talking when his phone rang. He said he had to take the call and excused himself. When he came back, he said his child was sick and he had to go home. I responded, "Okay, I hope he gets better," and he said, "Yeah, my wife told me." I was shocked. I said, "What?" He just looked at me, grabbed me, hugged me, gave me a kiss, and left. I was so hurt because I thought he was the one. I had my own Frankie Beverly. We spoke a few more times on the phone and even went out a few more times, but the word "wife" just didn't sit right with me, and I knew I had to end it. So I ended it. I'm not going to lie; I cried. Ladies, do your homework. Men, do your homework before getting into these situations. It makes sense that we went out of town a lot. He couldn't be seen locally with me. I said I was done dating. I did for eight months, and then I was dating again.

This time, I met a guy in a bakery shop. He liked what I had on. Of course, I liked the compliment. Ladies, it's nice to be complimented, but compliment yourself so you don't need validation from others. Love yourself, and every time you look in the mirror, affirm yourself with the word of God: Psalms 139:14 says, "I am fearfully and wonderfully made."

I don't remember how I ended up talking to this guy, but he turned out to be the absolute worst. He started off one way and then became a horrible individual who didn't believe in God. How in the world did I end up in this relationship? He caused so much damage to me and my children. He shoved me, yelled at me, and brought friends to my home to smoke crack cocaine. He had an illegal gun in my house and threatened me all the time. He wanted to fight my friends. It was just drama after drama, but I allowed it. I invited him into my home. I literally let the devil in. I never thought about it until now, but it was me who opened the door to the enemy. John 10:10 says, "The thief comes only to steal and kill and destroy," but he can only do that when we don't have our armor on, which is found in Ephesians 6:10-18. Had I been in the word like I was supposed to be, I would have recognized this enemy. I didn't use any of my weapons mentioned in Ephesians 6:10-18. Our lives should be placed under prayer so we can avoid a lot of unnecessary drama.

This relationship caused me to be sin-sick again. I stopped eating and sleeping. The sight of him literally made me sick. I went to the Lord in prayer. I repented and cried my eyes out, saying, "Please forgive me, remove this man from my life." His name was Dee too. What in the world is wrong with Dee's? I will never date a Dee ever again, period! I asked God to show me how to get rid of this man and remove him from my life forever.

A few days later, I came up with a plan. I pretended I couldn't afford to live in my place and told Dee # 2 I was moving. I got boxes and packed. I lived in a duplex house and rented out the basement. I told my roommate who lived upstairs about the crazy man. I told her it was all a fake, but I had to get this guy far away from me and my children. I asked her if my kids could stay with her until I got rid of him. She agreed, and I appreciate her to this day. Thank you Shay. We are the best of friends. I left to stay with my mom. I was so embarrassed and ashamed, but my mom never judged me. She understood, and I stayed with her for a while. I felt awful because I left my kids, but I had to do what I thought was best for them and me. I was living in fear. When you live in fear, it's another door open to the enemy. It keeps you in bondage, and you never walk in God's purpose. That's what the devil wants.

Dee # 2 knew I had moved in with my mom, and I wanted him to see that the fake move was official. As long as he knew I was with my mom, he wouldn't be around my children. Out of fear, I let him borrow my car, and of course, he let it get towed by parking in a tow zone. He didn't have the money to get it out. The bill was outrageous. I called the tow company, explained it was my car, and they said it was my lucky day. They discounted all the fees, and I only had to pay for the hook-up. I thanked the Lord and got my car back. As I was driving, I repented to the Lord again and said, "I am serious this time. When you remove this man from me, I will not date anyone unless you tell me." God heard my prayers to remove Dee # 2 out of my life by sentencing him to prison.

Chapter 9

The Musician

As you've read, my life hasn't been a bed of roses, and I've made many mistakes. I didn't tap into all that I've done and been through, that's not what's important. What's important is that we serve a God that knew we would fail. John 3:16 tells us, for God so loved the world that He sent His only begotten son that whosoever believes in Him should not perish but have everlasting life, for God sent not his son into the world to condemn the world but the world through Him might be saved. I want you to know that you are loved, you are enough, and you have been chosen by God despite all the bad decisions and mistakes. He went to the cross and laid down His life for us.

At one point, my daughter noticed that we weren't attending church like we used to. She said to me, "Mommy, we don't go to church like we used to," and that just broke my heart. At the time, we were living in Woodbridge, and my kids met a neighbor who lived at the end of our block. They invited my children to come to church and would even pick them up and take them there. I will never forget Miss

Vera and Mother Bessie, the sweetest people in the world, who just took my kids and loved on them. After my kids started attending church, I eventually began attending as well, though not regularly because I was working on Sundays.

I want to emphasize this: while we must work, it's important to honor God first by attending church. If you have to work, ask your employer to schedule you after your church service. Starting your week by going to the house of God sets the tone for the days ahead. Let your employer know that attending worship is important to you, and I know God will honor that. God can move your employer's heart to allow you to go to church on Sundays. We take our kids to so many places; let's make sure one of those places is church. You might feel the need to work, that you need the money, but I promise you, if you put God first, He will make a way for you. He will provide for you.

Hebrews 10:25 says, "Not forsaking the assembling of ourselves together, as the manner of some is, but exhorting one another, and so much the more as you see the day approaching." This verse reminds us of the importance of coming together to worship and praise God. Fellowship is crucial. I don't know about you, but every time I go to the house of worship, I feel better, even in the midst of all the mess I was in. So, please be intentional. If you don't have a church, find a local one that preaches the Word of God. Get yourself, your children, your family members, and your friends into the house of God.

As I started attending church more regularly, I joined the choir and the praise team. I was learning more about Christ, but I must be honest. I still hadn't applied God's Word to my life the way I should have. But I know that God kept His hand on me and never left me, even as I continued to make mistakes. When I made a mistake, I would repent and ask God for forgiveness, and then I'd strive and press on to be the best person I could be.

One Sunday, we had an evening service at our church. We didn't have any musicians, but there was a visitor who was a musician. He had attended the morning service, and during that time, he went up to the keyboard and played some songs. It was such a blessing to have someone play for us. As a choir and praise team, we did the best we could without a musician, but having one made such a difference. I approached the musician and asked if he could play for us that evening, but he told me he had an appointment with a real estate agent. I was persistent, though, and asked him again, saying, "Come on, sir, please. We need you to play for our choir." He finally agreed, and I was so happy. The song he played for us was "He's Able" by Kirk Franklin.

After that evening service, I noticed that this musician started attending our morning services regularly. I didn't even know his name at first, but once I recognized him, I asked if he would be willing to play for our choir regularly, and he agreed. He even began attending some of our rehearsals. We were so happy we could sing with music.

As he started coming to rehearsals regularly, I got a bit comfortable and asked if I could direct the choir. He told me he didn't see me as a choir director, that someone else would be better suited for the role. However, he did tell me that I had a gift for singing lead. I have to admit, I was in my feelings not directing, so I began to dislike our new musician because I couldn't direct the choir.

As time went on, we had some great rehearsals with our new musician. I can't remember what happened on one particular occasion, but I ended up needing a ride home from rehearsal. He overheard me talking about it and offered to give me a ride. After that ride, I started to like him again. I realized that sometimes we don't like hearing "no" or facing the truth. I didn't have a real reason to dislike him other than the fact that I couldn't get my way. Let's be honest. We've all been there. And know this, sometimes no is protection.

The ride home from choir rehearsals led to a good friendship. We shared a lot about our past experiences. I shared probably too much, talking about my promiscuous lifestyle, the clubs, the miscarriage, and the abortion; all things I probably should have kept to myself. But I wanted to be free. I had kept these things inside for so long, and now I realize that's why I was going out and dating the wrong people because of the shame and guilt I felt inside.

This is why it's so important to heal from the inside out. When you're wounded, you don't think straight; you fall for anything, and you compromise what you know is right to do wrong. Your mind needs to heal because a healed mind thinks differently and moves different.

There was something about this musician that allowed me to open up because I wanted to be accepted, not realizing that I was already accepted by Jesus who loves me in spite of my past. Why did I give myself and my time to all these people who didn't really love me? I felt comfortable talking to him because he listened and didn't judge. We both shared a lot of personal experiences and were both broken because of our past relationships. We would talk in the driveway for hours about our pasts.

Eventually, those rides home turned into dinner dates, and those dinner dates led to us becoming boyfriend and girlfriend—something neither of us wanted at the time. There was something different about this musician. I saw the love he had for God. Despite all his issues and problems, he never gave up on God and never stopped attending church, even after the rejection he faced from both the church and his family, as we discussed in our driveway conversations.

When we dated, we would go to church and then out to dinner, and I loved it. He was always dressed sharp, with eyeglasses to match every outfit and modest jewelry. This was different for me. One thing I learned about dating a musician is that people are attracted to them. Several women were attracted to my musician, and when they found out he had a girlfriend, they were upset. I was like, "Oh no, he's with me!" I remember one lady coming to church just to see him, and when she found out he was dating me, she left. Bye, Felicia! I thought it was funny.

On a serious note, the musician and I had one goal: we wanted to strengthen our relationship with Christ. We knew we needed to get serious about our spiritual lives.

Chapter 10

The Surprise Engagement

The Musician and I were at church during a praise and worship service. We started with "Thank You, Lord," and then, to my surprise, the next line sung by the Musician was, "Will you marry me?" It was the sweetest sound. He sang it again, "Will you marry me?" My answer was yes, but with one condition: as long as we take Jesus as our partner. So, we became engaged in January 2002.

I remember telling the Lord, "I don't want another relationship unless you approve." I wanted to break the cycle of multiple marriages that seemed to run in my family. This time, I knew God had approved because this marriage came through praise and worship. It never fails when you repent and pour out your heart to God with sincerity, He hears your prayers. I saw more than just a musician; I saw a true man of God wanted to build a relationship back to Christ. I saw the calling of a Pastor in him. This was exactly what I needed in my life. Because he had a desire to live for Christ, and God knew who I needed to be with to strengthen my relationship with God.

We got married in August 2002. The wedding was beautiful, though I still wonder why we wore black and gold in 98-degree weather lol. But it was all good. I just wish I had the chance to ride in a limo and dance at our reception. We had a lovely reception at a beautiful restaurant, but there was no dance floor lol. Our wedding was so special; the Musician played while I sang. Once I got the crackle out of my voice lol it was all good. We had about eight prayers, so we knew this marriage was going to last forever!

For our honeymoon, we went to Orlando, Florida, and Myrtle Beach. The children and my in-laws joined us, which worked out great because I had family to watch the kids. We had lots of fun at Universal Studios, riding roller coasters until the Incredible Hulk ride made me sick lol. That was the end of the rides for me.

After returning from the honeymoon, it was back to our 9-5 jobs. The Musician and I spent a lot of time working on music. We had a gospel go-go band with our kids and godchildren. We traveled a lot, and it was totally worth it to see the joy on people's faces when we ministered through music. Our vision was to plant a positive seed through music that would lead people, especially young people, to build a relationship with Jesus. When God gives you a gift, use it to glorify Him. As Colossians 3:23 says, "Whatever you do, work at it with all your heart, as working for the Lord, not for men."

A couple years after marriage, we were blessed with a son. I must admit, we were surprised! Our little baby boy brought so much joy to our family, and having older siblings really helped. We named him Elias. He was a good baby, though he didn't sleep through the night. As he grew, we felt the need to purchase a home. We moved to a rural area that was nice and quiet. However, after a year and a half, both my husband and I were laid off, and we lost the house. We had to surrender our vehicles because we couldn't afford them. I would advise anyone to put 3 to 6 months of income aside because you never know what may happen.

I was devastated, depressed, and mad all at the same time. My emotions were all over the place. My husband and I searched for jobs, but nothing was available at the time. It was during this difficult period that my husband told me the Lord spoke to him about starting a church. I couldn't believe it! We were losing our house and cars, and he wanted to start a church? I asked, "Where is the money going to come from to start a church?" I was really upset with him because he's wanting to start a church. I saw the calling of his life but I was saying in my head, "Now Lord?"

A few days later, my husband, the Musician, went out and found a church. He saw a sign that said "new location," found the old location, met the Pastor, and next thing I knew, we had a church with no money down. The Pastor just gave my husband the key. I knew it was God when my husband came back home and told me. I felt pretty bad because I wasn't ready to be a Pastor's wife—me, the First Lady! I didn't have any big hats or fancy clothes. I didn't feel like I fit the position, mostly because of my past. But God reminded me that I am the righteousness of God, redeemed, and my sins have been forgiven.

We started in a friend's basement; thank you to the Hudson's; until the other church relocated. My husband and I were ordained. I am now the First Lady of Chosen Ministries. Everyone thinks the First Lady's job is just to look pretty, but it's much more than that. The First Lady has to help her husband run the ministry, pray at all times, smile even when she knows people are talking about the pastor, and be an ear when the pastor needs to vent. First Ladies have to be strong, supportive, and encouraging; they're the real backbone. They stand by their husbands when everyone else walks away from the church. I am that First Lady!

Everything I went through prepared me for ministry. God's grace really is sufficient. I really am CHOSEN.

Chapter 11

An Unexpected Visit

As you may have read in the trial, I was fortunate not to receive any jail time, but I was given probation and ordered to pay restitution.

One morning, we received an unexpected knock at the door. When I opened it, I was greeted by U.S. Marshals holding up a badge, asking for LaJuanda. I told them, "I am her." One of them said, "There's been a warrant out for your arrest for years." Stunned, I asked, "What is the warrant for?" The U.S. Marshal replied, "Violation of probation." I was shocked and explained, "I was on probation 10 years ago, and I completed it. I have the documents to prove it." He responded, "Ma'am, I'm sorry, but we have to take you in."

In disbelief, I called my husband, who was in the bedroom at the time, and told him what was happening. There was nothing he could do. The U.S. Marshals took me to Woodbridge. Then I was transferred to another vehicle to Fairfax country. I cried uncontrollably until I vomited, forcing the officers to pull over and let me finish throwing up outside the car. This was, by far, the worst day I had ever experienced. In my mind, I was saying, "Lord, I've repented. I will never do anything against your will. I'm loving your people, and yet this happens."

When we arrived at the police station, they checked me in, took my fingerprints, and mugshot, and placed me in a holding area. I was still crying because I had to leave my family behind. My little Elias was only 3 or 4 years old, and I was wondering what he would think if Mommy wasn't there. Let me say this to anyone reading: when you sin, it affects everyone around you. It puts strain and worry on your family. My little toddler was asking for his mommy—how do you explain to your little one that Mommy is in jail? How do you tell anyone? It's hard. Please think and ask yourself, "Will God be pleased if I do this?" Even though I had asked for forgiveness and was forgiven, there were still consequences.

I was held in a correctional center for 3 days. I was in a cell with all kinds of women—addicts, alcoholics, and those who stole to get money for their drug use. What surprised me was that many of them were middle-class women, married with jobs. They were so broken and damaged that substance abuse was their coping mechanism. We would all talk and ask each other, "Why are you here?" When I shared my story, they were all surprised. They said, "You're one of the good ones; you won't be in here long." I told them, "We all sin and fall short of the glory of God. It's in Romans 3:23. But God loves you." Although these women were married, none of them felt loved by their families because their spouses never affirmed them or made them feel valued. This showed me that we must be careful how we treat God's children. We are all His children. I encouraged the women to join a church or a prayer group where they could start to clean up their lives, and if they needed rehabilitation, that was okay too. I told them, "Just know Jesus loves you."

After one day in the holding area, I was called to be assigned to a cell. I started crying again and again. I cried so much that they moved me to another cell because they thought I was suicidal. I heard the officers talking about me. They were concerned, saying they had never seen anyone cry the way I was crying. I wasn't suicidal; I just wanted to get out of that place and return home to my family. The next day, I had to appear in court. When they called my name, they asked, "Why did you violate your probation?" I replied, "I completed it." Then they explained, "You haven't completed paying your restitution." I responded, "Oh!" They pulled records showing that I was paying, but it wasn't enough. The judge suggested I pay more. I asked him, "Can we drop the interest charges? That's why it looks like I'm not paying enough." He agreed, and my family helped to ensure this would not happen again. But guess what? It happened again. Another warrant for the same thing—violation of probation. I couldn't believe it. I was paying my restitution. This time, the warrant was left on my door, so my husband took me to the police station, thinking it must be a mistake. When I turned myself in, I thought I would be going back home in a couple of hours. But they kept me. The look on my husband's face is one I will never forget. He was in total shock. I had to go to jail for 2 days, but this time was different. I didn't cry—I gained strength, which I know God gave me. I started to minister to the women and prayed with them. I was even teaching Bible study. The women didn't want me to leave. You know what's funny? Before all of this happened, I had asked God to equip me on how to minister to hurting women. I laughed to myself and thought, "God, did I have to come here to jail? Couldn't You have picked a restaurant or a mall?"

This time, we hired a bondsman and a lawyer. After two days, I was released on bond. When it was time for my next court date, the violation of probation was due to not notifying the probation department of my new address. My attorney said, "Well, how did the U.S. Marshals know where she lived? All her money orders have her current address, and her probation officer has documents supporting that she notified them of the move." The judge dropped the charge, saying, "This case is too old. We are closing it, and I don't want to see this case again." I said, "Thank you, Jesus, and thank you, Judge."

Let me tell you something I've learned in my walk with Christ. The devil comes to steal, kill, and destroy according to John 10:10. He is always seeking to destroy your character after you have changed your heart and mind to serve Christ. He tries to discourage you and make you think you should have stayed in the world's system instead of surrendering to God's way and His will. But 1 Peter 4:12 says, "Beloved, think it not strange concerning the fiery trial which is to try you, as though some strange thing happened unto you: But rejoice, inasmuch..." In other words, endure trials with faith and hope.

The enemy knows that with Jesus, we are already victorious in everything. Every situation we face, we will win. Be encouraged and always remember 2 Corinthians 4:17: "For our light affliction, which is but for a moment, worketh for us a far more exceeding and eternal weight of glory."

Chapter 12

Three Months of Pain

In 2014, I experienced significant physical changes in my body. I was extremely tired, developed skin rashes, lost weight, had fevers, and felt incredibly stressed. I wanted to sleep all the time and had no energy; even walking was painful. I visited multiple doctors who told me I was anemic and suggested taking iron pills, but despite following their advice, my symptoms persisted for several months. I found myself in the emergency room frequently, always hearing the same diagnosis: anemia.

One day, despite feeling terribly sick, I kept a hair appointment— something I was very particular about. I shared my symptoms with my hairdresser, who recommended that I see her primary care doctor. I'm so glad I took her advice. I managed to get an emergency appointment, and after the assistant took my temperature and vitals, the doctor immediately sent me to the ER. Once there lab work revealed that my hemoglobin had dropped to a dangerously low level of 2, and I needed a blood transfusion right away. I was admitted to the hospital and stayed for several days until my hemoglobin levels improved, then I was released to go home.

For a few weeks, I felt a bit better, but soon the symptoms of extreme tiredness, low energy, and body aches returned—this time with higher fevers. I went back to the ER, where my hemoglobin levels had dropped again, requiring another blood transfusion. They conducted more tests and confirmed that I had severe anemia. I was released again, but the symptoms persisted. It felt like I had a severe case of the flu.

On the day my family and I were preparing to attend my uncle's funeral, I felt chills, pain, and discomfort on our way there. My husband noticed and asked if I was okay. I told him, "Babe, we have to get me to the hospital, or we'll be attending my funeral." He rushed me to the ER. Upon arrival, my fever was at 103, and it wouldn't go down. Further tests showed that my kidneys were shutting down, my white blood count was extremely low, my blood pressure was high, and my hemoglobin levels were critically low again. The doctor said I had arrived just in time, and I was admitted once more needing another blood transfusion.

It was December 2014. The doctors ran numerous tests because they suspected that there was more to my condition than anemia. Then, I started having seizures. I remember watching TV in the hospital room, seeing blurred lines crossing the screen, not realizing it was a seizure. Apparently, they worsened, and a nurse, who was off duty, felt compelled to check on me before she left. It was the Holy Spirit guiding her (God was covering me even when I wasn't in control). She found me having a seizure and immediately called my husband, who rushed back to the hospital. The seizures became so severe that they transferred me to VCU Hospital. I don't remember much of this, but my husband told me that the seizures intensified, and they had to induce me into a medical coma, telling my family I might not make it through the night.

This moment was incredibly hard on my family. My husband had to work and take care of our youngest son. During this time, while I was in the hospital, my mother-in-law and a close friend who had been responsible for taking my kids to church passed away. My family didn't tell me at the time because there was so much going on. I don't remember much about those three months in the hospital, but I do know that my son, Dante, stayed right by my side the entire time.

After a month the doctors diagnosed me with Systemic Lupus Erythematosus (SLE), an autoimmune disease that attacks any part of the body. In my case, Lupus affected my brain, heart, kidneys, nervous system, skin, joints, and lungs. I had to relearn how to walk, write, and use my hands. It was a challenge, but God got me through it. I was also diagnosed with Lymphoma, but after a few weeks, the cancer was gone. And one day, this Lupus will be gone too. God has been so good to me, He's never failed me. Try Him for yourself. If He did it for me, He will do it for you. The same God right now is the same God back then. Give your life to Him. You may think you're waiting on God, but He's really waiting on you. Life will come with challenges but we have a savior who will deliver us.

I am so grateful that God has allowed me to share my testimony with you. I pray that you are encouraged. Remember this: "Now thanks be to God who always leads us in triumph in Christ, and maketh manifest the savor of his knowledge by us in every place." (2 Corinthians 2:14)

A Prayer for You

Father God, in the Name of Jesus, I come to You this day and thank You for being God in my life. Thank You for grace & mercy that covered me when I was doing what I wanted and not be attentive to Your Words and instructions You had for me. Your Word tells me that You know the plans for my life, which is to prosper and not to harm me but to give me a hope and a future filled with abundance and overflow of blessings. Forgive me for all the times I did not trust You but leaned to my own understanding. Your Word is a lamp unto my feet that will guide me into greatness. Old things shall be passed away and I will become a new creature in Christ because I have been bought with a price. You have redeemed me and my mind is transformed to be Christ-like. No weapon formed against me shall prosper because I belong to You. You are Lord of my life and no good thing will You withhold from me!

In Jesus' Name, Amen.

Scriptures To Encourage You

Jeremiah 29:11

"For I know the plans I have for you, declares the Lord, plans to prosper you and not harm you, plans to give you hope and a future."

Psalms 139:14

"I praise you because I am fearfully and wonderfully made."

Isaiah 54:17

"No weapon that is formed against you will succeed, and every tongue that rises against you in judgment you will condemn."

1 Corinthians 6:20

"You were bought with a price. You were actually purchased with the precious blood of Jesus and made His own."

Psalms 119:105

"Your Word is a lamp to my feet and a light to my path."

John 3:16

"For God so loved the world that He gave His only begotten Son, that whosoever believeth in Him should not perish, but have everlasting life."

1 John 1:9

"If we confess our sins, He is faithful and just to forgive us our sins, and to cleanse us from all unrighteousness."

Romans 10:9

"If you confess with your mouth that Jesus is Lord and believe in your heart that God raised Him from the dead, you will be saved."

Ephesians 2:10

"For we are God's masterpiece. He has created us anew in Christ Jesus, so we can do the good things He planned for us long ago."

1 John 4:19

"We love because He first loved us."

Philippians 4:13

"I can do all things through Christ who gives me strength."

Affirm Yourself

I am free from all guilt and shame

I forgive myself

I am fearfully and wonderfully made

I am healed

I am strong

I am thankful

I am redeemed

I am chosen

I am God's masterpiece

I am loved by God

I can do all things through Christ who strengthens me.

God's strength is made perfect in weakness

I am a new creation

I am courageous

Thank You!

Thank you Jesus for being the author and finisher of my life and never letting me go!

Thank you to:

My wonderful supportive husband who loves me unconditionally, my protector and my covering, you pushed me to another level in my spiritual walk, your guidance taught me how to defeat the enemy through praise and worship and now we do ministry together spreading the gospel through song and teaching.

I love you Babe! Because of you I wear the Title "First Lady "

Thanks to My Parents, you are the best . Your love is just like God's you will never know how proud I am to be your daughter. Even when I disappointed you at times you never made me feel unloved. Thank you to my bonus parents who always treated me like I was your biological child.

Thank you to my 3 Children whom God allowed me to give birth to. The best gifts other than Jesus.

I am so blessed and honored you call me Mommy!

Thank you to the Late Dr. Rudyne Sherfield who taught me how to be a wife.

Thank you to my Son in Law who loves my daughter.

Thank you to my bonus kids who love me and treat me so good.

Thank you to all my siblings, I love you from the bottom of my heart and my sisters who typed and carried the blue bag with all the pages to this book.

Thank you Constance Mama C. Watson for giving me a microphone.

Thank you to the Overseer Diane Ford, I was restored through your Ministry along with The Late Apostle Mitchell Ford

Thank you Apostle Mother Woods and to the Late Apostle Eric Woods for giving me the assignment this book was birthed from your conference.

Thank you Lakeya Hunt owner of Inspire Selections Boutique for keeping me well dressed as the First Lady.

Thank you Tania Johnson for slaying my hair.

Thank you Chosen Ministries for your love and support.

Last but not least

Thank you Whittney Kilgore I call you my "Enforcer "God put you in my life at the right time.You held me accountable to getting this book completed.

Thank you to everyone who took time to read this book.

Love you,

First Lady

www.ingramcontent.com/pod-product-compliance
Lightning Source LLC
Chambersburg PA
CBHW051554120626
46551CB00013B/1508